Men's Fashion Illustrations from the Turn of the Century

BY JNO. J. MITCHELL CO.

Selected and with an Introduction by

JEAN L. DRUESEDOW

Associate Curator-in-Charge
The Costume Institute
The Metropolitan Museum of Art

DOVER PUBLICATIONS, INC.
New York

Men's Fashion Illustrations from the Turn of the Century is a new
work, first published by Dover Publications, Inc., in 1990.

DOVER *Pictorial Archive* SERIES

This book belongs to the Dover Pictorial Archive Series. You may
use the designs and illustrations for graphics and crafts applications,
free and without special permission, provided that you include no more than
ten in the same publication or project. (For permission for additional use,
please write to Dover Publications, Inc., 31 East 2nd Street, Mineola, N.Y. 11501.)
However, republication or reproduction of any illustration by any other
graphic service whether it be in a book or in any other design resource is strictly prohibited.

Manufactured in the United States of America
Dover Publications, Inc.
31 East 2nd Street
Mineola, N.Y. 11501

Library of Congress Cataloging-in-Publication Data

Men's fashion illustrations from the turn of the century.

(Dover pictorial archive series)
Reprint. Originally published: New York : Jno. J. Mitchell Co., 1910.
1. Costume—History—19th century. 2. Fashion—History—19th century.
I. Druesedow, Jean L. II. Jno. J. Mitchell Co. III. Series.
GT595.M46 1990   391′.1′09041   90-3198
ISBN 0-486-26353-3

Introduction

Firmly convinced that nothing we can do is too good for our subscribers, and that no excellence we attain in our work is unappreciated by them, and knowing that nothing contributes more to our own satisfaction than to surpass our best previous efforts, especially in the art direction, we make a new departure this month in fashion reporting.

The Sartorial Art Journal, July 1903

This enthusiastic statement captures the buoyant pride of the journal, a trade magazine serving the Merchant Tailors' National Protective Association specifically and the trade in general. The Jno. J. Mitchell Publishing Company had begun publication of the *The Sartorial Art Journal* in 1874, offering tailor's supplies (not cloth but tools), patented measuring devices, patterns and fashion plates. In July 1905 it announced the thirty-first volume in glowing terms

The Sartorial Art Journal has steadily expanded through thirty volumes from a single number of little more than pamphlet size to a bulk that averages each month about one hundred pages from cover to cover, and from two or three small diagrams to from eight to ten full page diagrams and illustrations; and special features and new departments have been added to it until it now includes full and authoritative information about everything of interest to merchant tailors and cutters from current fashions to how to exemplify them practically, from correct tailor-made garments for social functions, general wear, outing, sporting, uniforms and liveries to the minutest details of the dress accessories, and from the epoch-making organized movements of the trade to what individual tailors of prominence are doing. The plates of fashion which form, of course, the most important part of the publication, have increased in number of illustrations until sometimes those of one month would have amply sufficed for the corresponding months of from three to four years until less than ten years ago, and for an entire year until its tenth volume was completed.

A selection of the "plates of fashion" that appear in the journal between 1900 and 1910 is the basis of this book. The plates span the period of masculine style dominated by Edward VII of England, whose brief reign lasted from 1901 to 1910. They reflect the spirit, as well as the silhouette, of the portly English monarch in their depiction of fashionable men of affairs who seem fully aware of the importance of appropriate behavior and dress. No one was more meticulous in these matters than Edward himself.

Large-format fashion illustrations were issued as a supplement to *The Sartorial Art Journal* for tailors to use in consulting with clients in order to determine the finer points of style in bespoke (made-to-order) garments. The journal itself reproduced smaller versions of these illustrations, along with descriptions of the fabrics shown, flat-pattern drafts and advice concerning suitable occasions for wearing the garments. In April 1905, the editors were pleased to point out that

> everything we illustrate is first sketched from the thing itself and that the thing itself is the product of some high class metropolitan tailoring establishment that has kindly loaned it to us for that special purpose; the novelties we illustrate are not experiments but new things that men of high reputation are wearing; the ultra styles are emanations from the cultivated but sometimes daring tastes of tailors of high standing, who number among their customers men who are acknowledged leaders in exclusive social circles; and the conservative things are always unimpeachably correct as they are faithful representations of costumes that were made by some house of high standing for some of its socially most highly esteemed and sartorially most influential customers.

An example of "ultra" style can be seen in a plate reproduced here from September 1901 (p. 28). Only an experienced tailor would have realized that this was "the latest and most extreme style of the cutaway frock," for often the difference in style from season to season was in the distance between buttons or in the distance between the top button and the neck, or whether the coat skirts were squared or curved at the center front. Elaborate descriptions and measurements in conjunction with the flat-pattern drafts revealed these subtleties, of which this same "ultra" cutaway furnishes an excellent example.

> CUTAWAY FROCK SUIT—The materials represented are a cheviot for the coat and a fancy worsted for the vest for the front view and a cheviot suiting for back view.
>
> THE COAT—The lengths are 18¾ and from 38 to 39 inches for a man of average height, 5 feet 8 inches. . . . The gorge is moderately high and long, the notch widths are each 1¼″ and the roll is 5 inches long. There are five buttons and buttonholes below the roll; but the fronts close with four buttons.

Instructions for drafting the flat pattern to size were given both in inches (called "short measures" by the journal) and by references indicating the proportions of such measurements to the chest measurement. For example, the sleeve fullness at the armscye for this coat (called the "working power" by the journal) is described as "2 inches less than one half the full breast size, 18 inches for this draft." Such highly complex technical descriptions were, of course, the language of the trade, and the tailor would know just how to adjust the draft measurements to fit his customer.

The largest group of plates in this volume has been chosen from the year 1900. For subsequent years the selection is based on both repetition and novelty, for we hope to show the continuity of Edwardian male dress as well as examples of variations in cut and accessories as they were published. One example of continuity is the short topcoat worn by the figure at the right in Plate A of May 1900 (p. 9). In October 1901 (p. 27), the same coat is described as a "Street Covert. The material represented is a covert coating. The average length is 34 inches." It appears again in October 1902 (p. 41), November 1903 (p. 53) and January 1906 (p. 73). The most noticeable variations occur in the types of sack suits and their accessories. Such suits played an increasingly important role in the well-dressed man's wardrobe, eventually replacing the frock coat and cutaway as correct business and street apparel.

Appropriate locations for wearing these fashions are indicated by the backgrounds chosen for the illustrations. For example, Plate B from the issue of January 1900 (p. 2) shows coaching costumes, Plate B of September 1900 (p. 14) juxtaposes formal household livery (the butler's brass buttons and horizontally striped vest) with the gentleman's full evening dress; Plate A of July 1901 (p. 25) illustrates what could be worn on and around yachts and related social events, while Plate B for that month (p. 26) depicts an evening at a summer resort. The description for Plate B calls tuxedo jackets "Summer Dress Negligee Costumes," reporting that they have become more acceptable for formal occasions and are grudgingly acknowledged to be acceptable for "stag parties, at the theatre and even at dinner parties and dances in summer resorts except when these are of the most formal character."

In looking at the backgrounds, those readers familiar with New York City and its history will recognize those landmarks that stand today (the Columbus Monument, p. 22; Grant's Tomb, p. 31; Bethesda Fountain, p. 38) and those that have vanished (the *Herald* Building, p. 5; the Vanderbilt houses, p. 41; the old Waldorf-Astoria, p. 42).

Apart from the plates and their descriptions, *The Sartorial Art Journal* offered articles of general interest to the trade and space for advertising. An article of October 1908 addressed the comparative values of custom-made and ready-to-wear clothing—an issue of real concern to individual tailors. Needless to say, the editor supported his constituency:

> A very important difference between custom-made and ready-to-wear clothes is that the former may be expressive of the wearer's mind, not only in an art direction, but as regards sartorial utility and appropriateness, whereas the latter express only the ideas and views of the designer plus, perhaps, those of his employer and associates.
>
> A self-respecting man of good taste and right views about propriety as regards his outward presentation of himself should feel, and generally does, as uncomfortable in clothes that he selects for himself ready to wear, no matter what their excellence may be as clothes, as any right-thinking man should feel were he compelled to subscribe to doctrines he does not comprehend, or to express his opinions in language prescribed by law.

The second annual convention of the Merchant Tailors' National Protective Association was fully reported in the April 1905 issue, which included discussions of labor problems between the merchant tailors and the unions representing their employees; an increase in the annual assessment of association dues; the advantages gained by large tailoring establishments, which could avoid middlemen or jobbers and thus buy goods direct from the mills at rates far below those of the small tailor; a report on the Old Tailors' Home; a "lengthy" paper on publicity and advertising; a discussion of modern business methods; reports from local organizations and individuals and a series of resolutions and amendments to the association's by-laws. The delegates posed for a group picture and attended an elaborate banquet featuring seven entertaining after-dinner toasts and speeches.

Local association events were also reported, such as a picnic of the St. Louis Custom Cutters' Association on July 24, 1909, when a baseball game between the Woolen and Trimming Salesmen and the Tailors and Cutters ended with a score of 17–6 for the salesmen. Photographs of the organizing committee, the teams and the trophy were reproduced with a detailed account of the game in the September 1909 journal.

The Sartorial Art Journal merged with *American Tailor and Cutter*, another trade publication, in 1916. In 1929 it merged again to become *The American Gentleman and*

Sartorial Art Journal. As American Mitchell Fashion Publishers, the company produced *American Ladies' Tailor* and *Men's Modes*. The last copyright held by the company was sold to Master Designer, a Chicago publishing firm which continues to publish *Frank C. Doblin's Modern Mitchell System of Men's Designing*, the only current publication to retain the Mitchell name in the title.

There can be no doubt that the study of *The Sartorial Art Journal* reveals a unique view of the tailor's trade and the tailor's clients. I am indebted to Robert Kaufmann, Associate Museum Librarian in the Irene Lewisohn Costume Reference Library of the Costume Institute at The Metropolitan Museum of Art, for providing this group of fashion plates and helping in their selection, and for sharing with me his own enthusiasm for the journal for which they were originally commissioned. A close study of the plates reproduced here, together with their wonderful depictions of the context for fashion and fashionable attitudes, emphasizes the great subtlety and elegance of Edwardian sartorial art.

JEAN L. DRUESEDOW
October 1989

B

Copyright
The Jno. J. Mitchell Co.
March 1900

MARCH 1900   3

FIFTH AVENUE

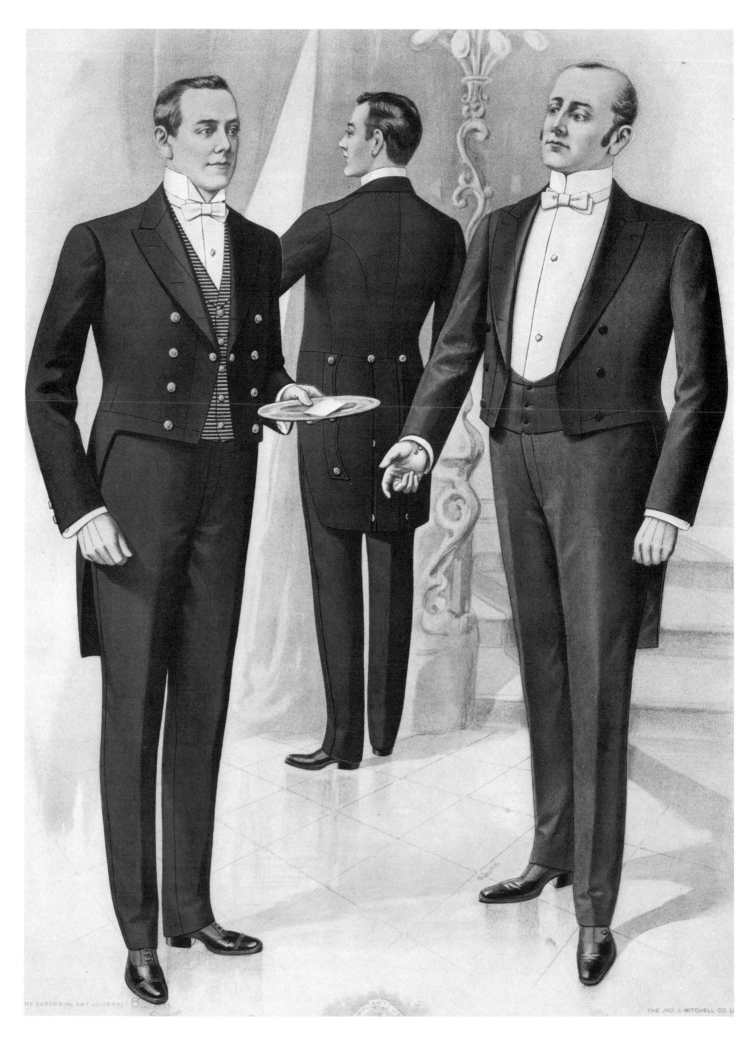

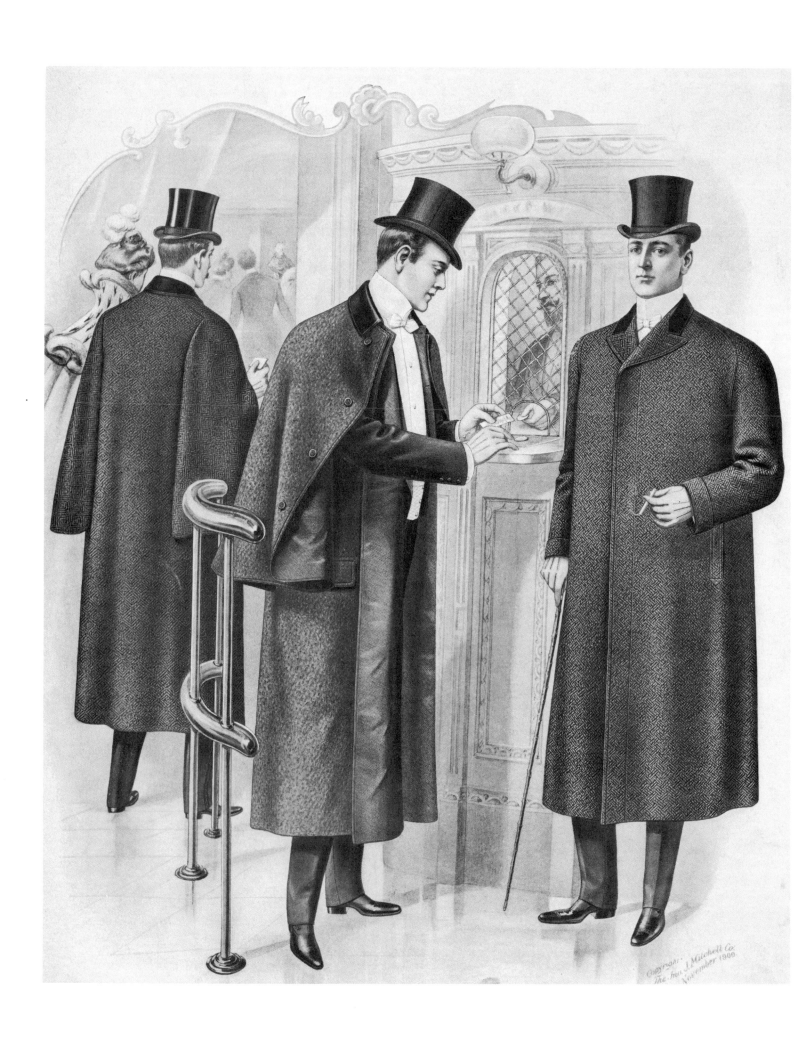

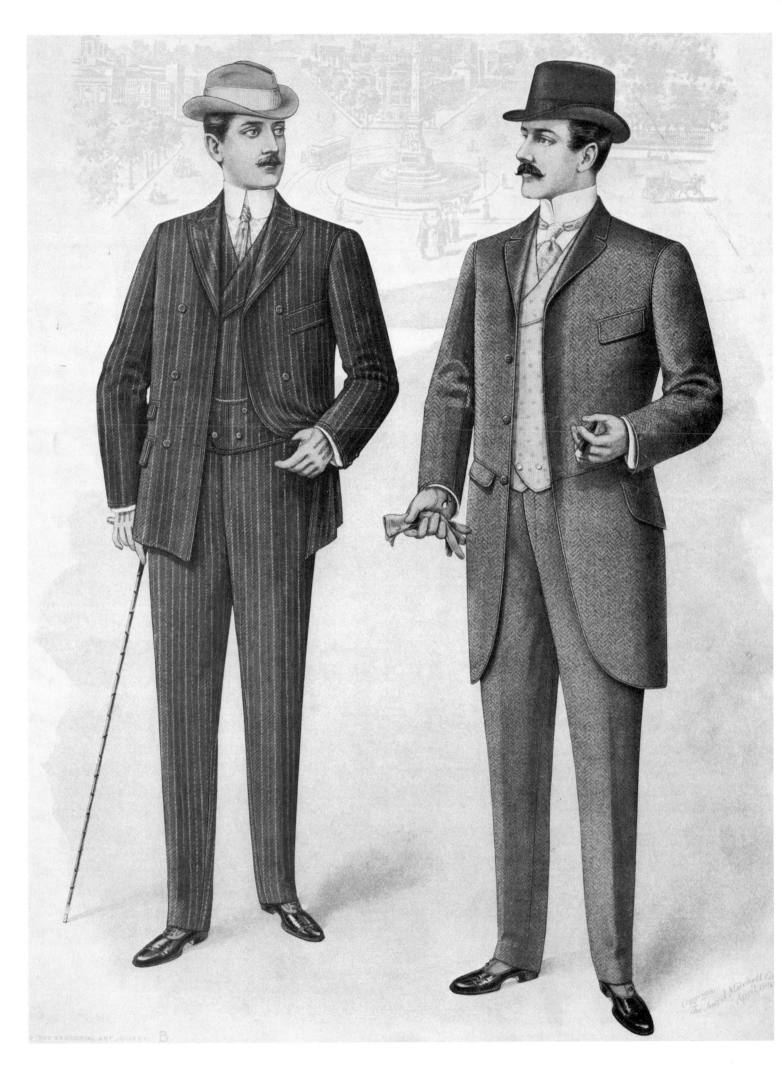

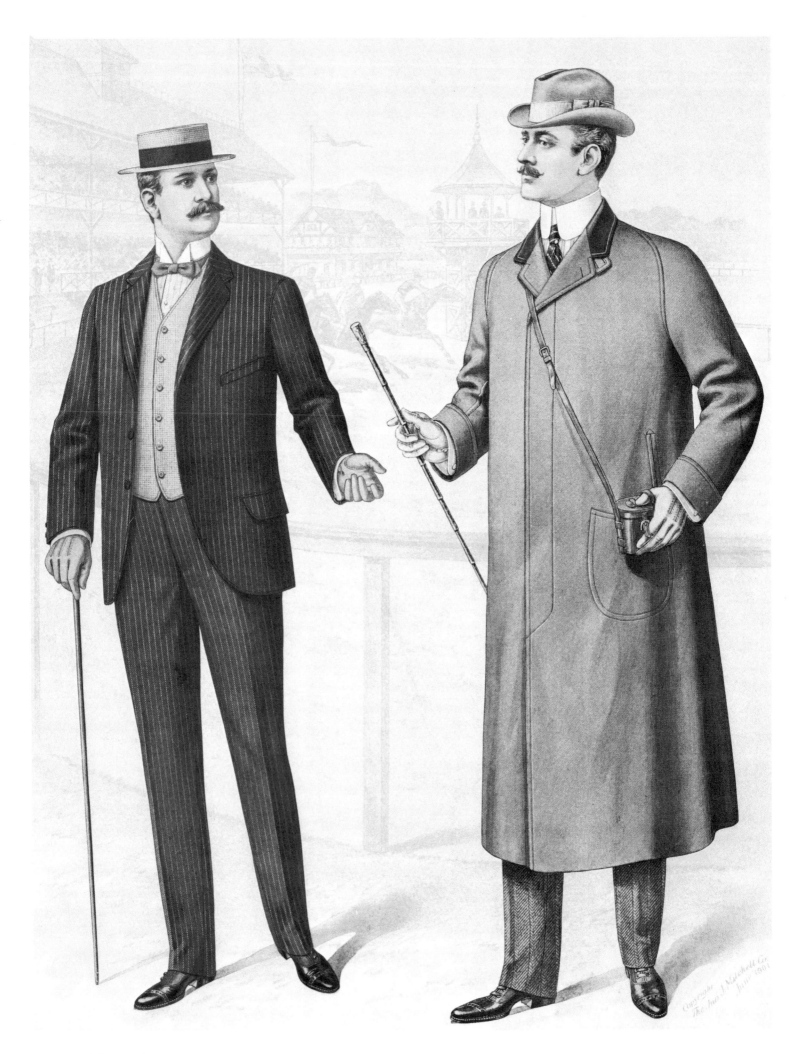

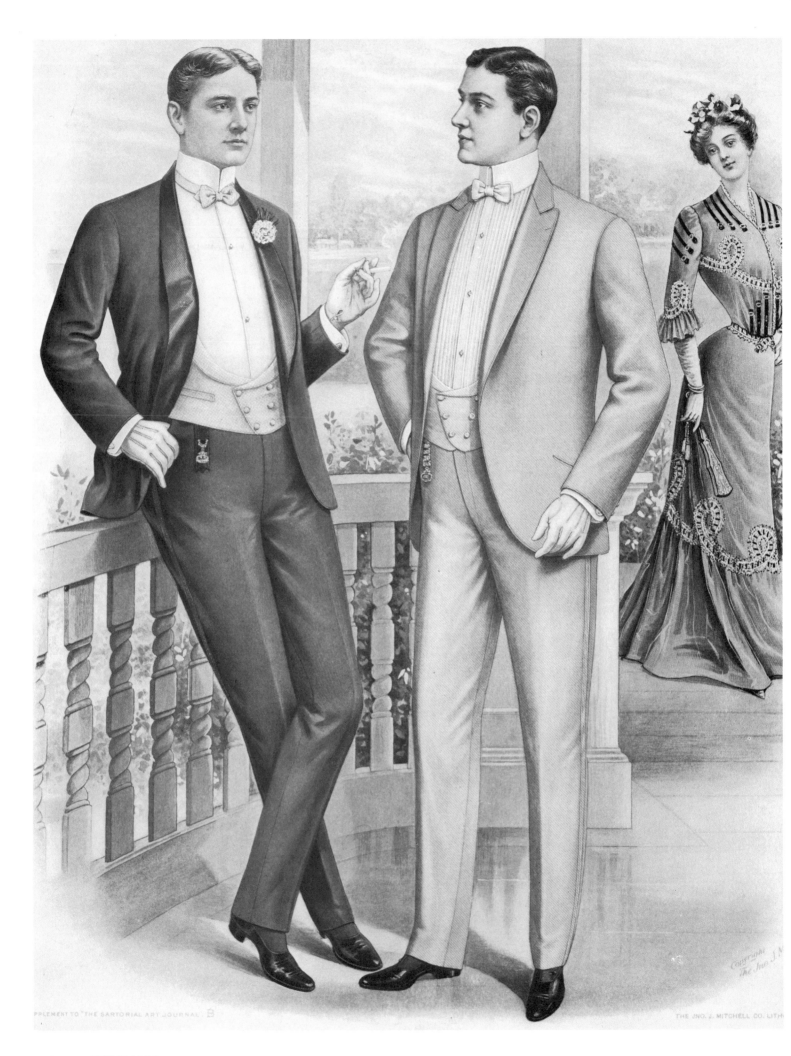

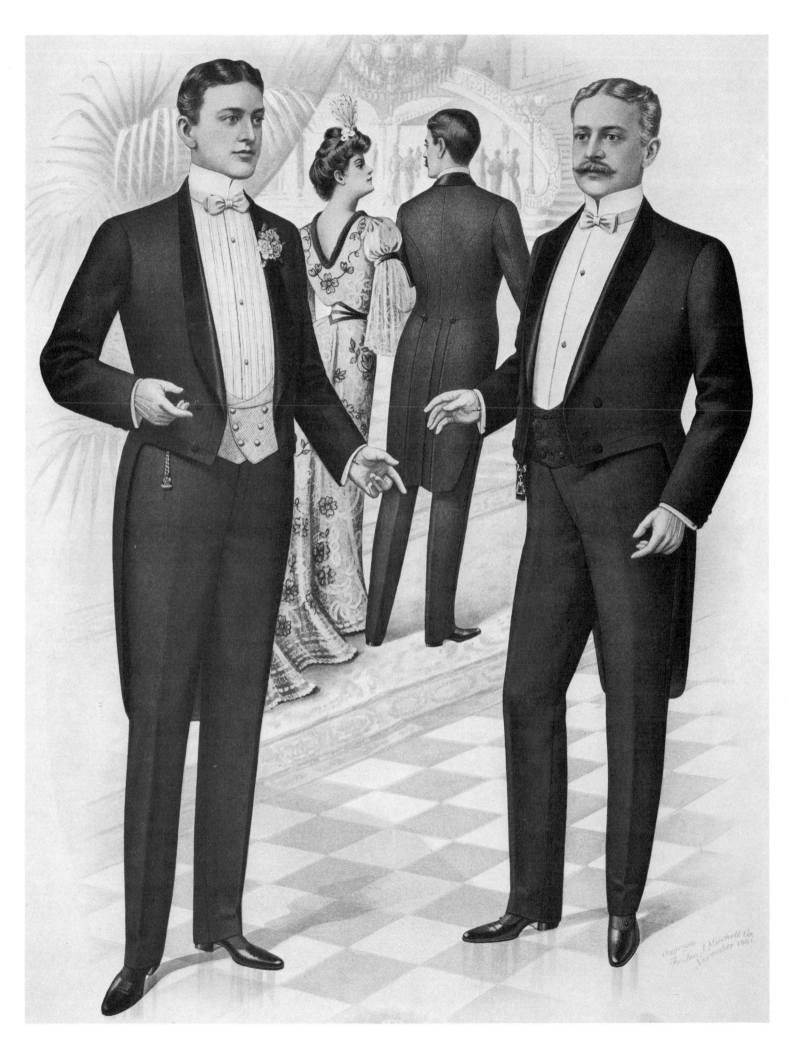

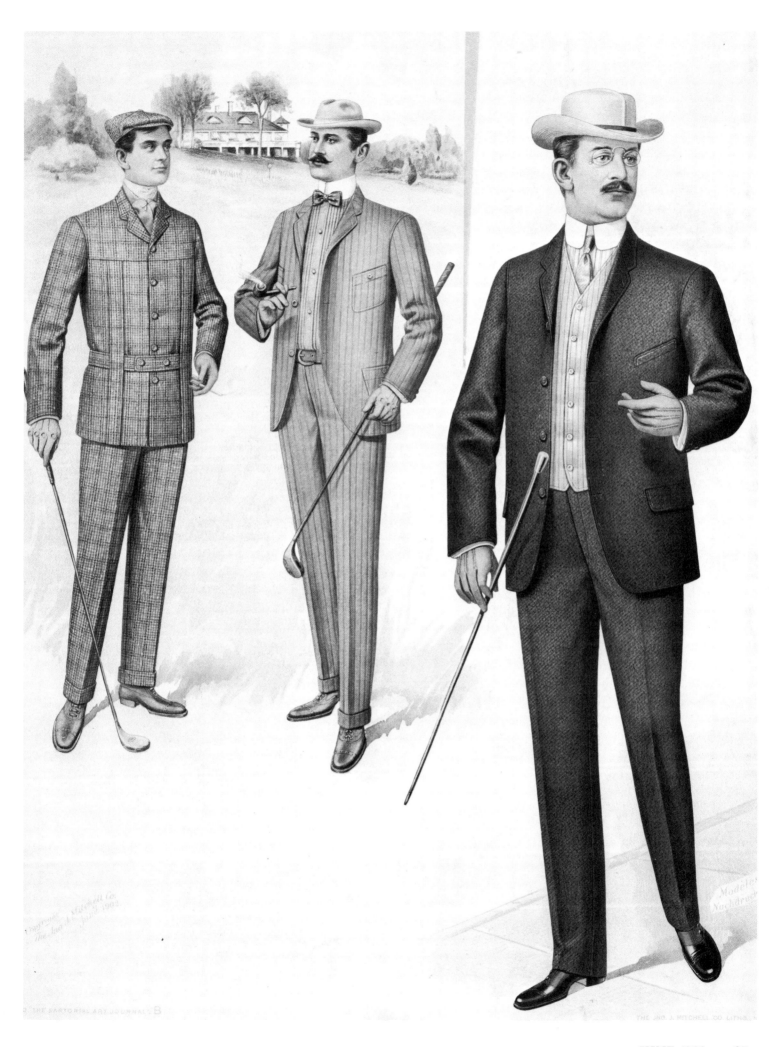

Copyright
the Jno. J. Mitchell Co.
October 1902

THE JNO. J. MITCHELL CO. LITHO, NEW YORK.

Copyright,
The Jno. J. Mitchell Co.
October 1902

Copyright
The Jno. J. Mitchell Co.
March 1903

Modèles Déposés
Nachdruck Verboten.

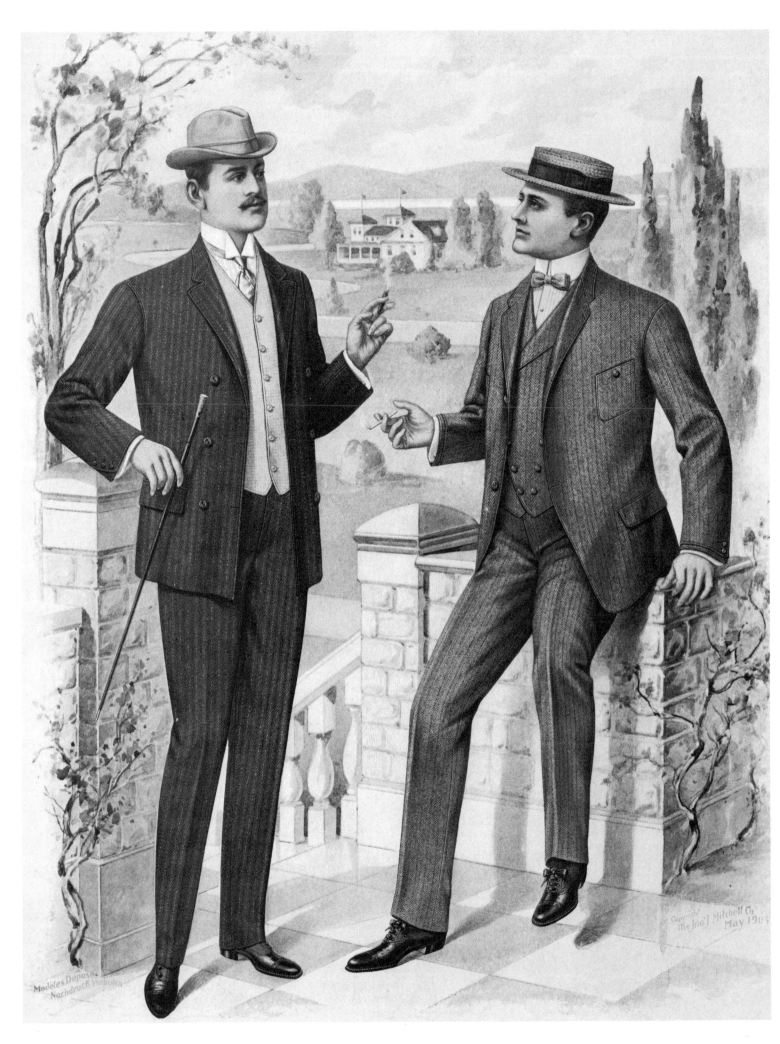

Modèles Déposés
Nachdruck Verboten

Copyright
The Jno. J. Mitchell Co.
April 1904

Modèles Déposés
Nachdruck Verboten

Copyright
The Jno J. Mitchell Co
MAY 1904

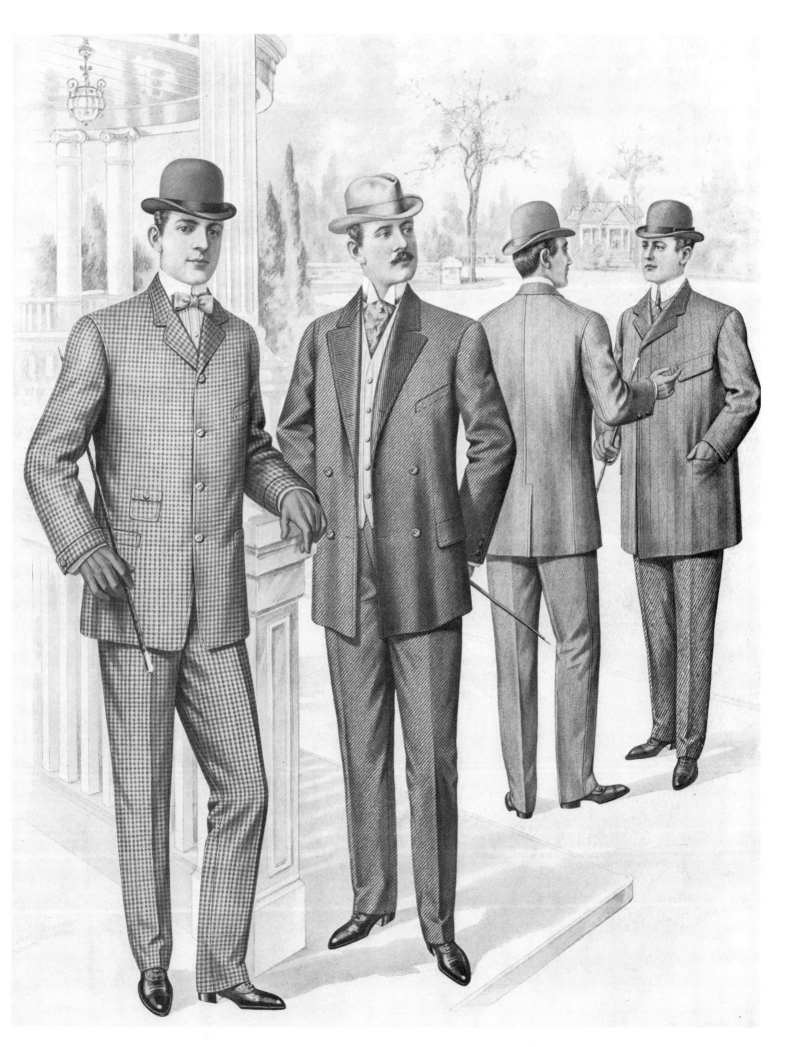

Copyright 1906
the Jno J. Mitchell Co.

Modeles Deposes
Nachdruck Verboten

Copyright 1906
The Jno. J. Mitchell Co.

Modèles Deposés
Nachdruck Verboten

Copyright 1906
the Jno J Mitchell Co.

Copyright 1906
the Jno. J. Mitchell Co.

Modeles Deposes
Nachdruck Verboten

Modèles Déposés
Nachdruck Verboten

Copyright 1906
The Jno. J. Mitchell Co.

Modèles Déposés
Nacharuck Verboten

Copyright 1908
The Jno. J. Mitchell Co.

Modèles Déposés
Nachdruck Verboten

Copyright 1907
The Jno. J. Mitchell Co.

Copyright 1908
The Jno. J. Mitchell Co.

Modèles Déposés
Nachdruck Verboten.

Copyright 1908
The Jno J Mitchell Co.

Modéles Déposés
Nachdruck Verboten.

Copyright 1908
The Jno. J. Mitchell Co.

Modeles Deposes
Nachdruck Verboten

Copyright 1908
by Jno. J. Mitchell Co.

Modéles Déposés
Nachdruck Verboten

Copyright 1908
The Jno. J. Mitchell

Copyright 1909
The Jno. J. Mitchell Co.

Copyright 1909
The Jno. J. Mitchell Co.